Japan

Julie McCulloch

**Heinemann
Library**

Chicago, Illinois

© 2001 Reed Educational & Professional Publishing
Published by Heinemann Library,
an imprint of Reed Educational & Professional Publishing,
Chicago, IL

Customer Service 888-454-2279

Visit our website at www.heinemannlibrary.com

Designed by Tinstar Design
Illustrations by Nicholas Beresford-Davies
Originated by Dot Gradations
Printed by Wing King Tong in Hong Kong

05 04 03 02 01
10 9 8 7 6 5 4 3 2 1

Library of Congress Cataloging-in-Publication Data
McCulloch, Julie, 1973-
    Japan / Julie McCulloch.
        p. cm. -- (A world of recipes)
    Includes bibliographical references and index.
    ISBN 1-58810-087-1 (library binding)
    1. Cookery, Japanese--Juvenile literature. [1. Cookery, Japanese. 2. Japan--Social life and customs.] I. Title.

TX724.5.J3 M38 2001
641.5952--dc21

                                    00-059748

Acknowledgments

The Publishers would like to thank the following for permission to reproduce photographs:
Robert Harding, p.5. All other photographs: Gareth Boden.
Illustration p.45, US Department of Agriculture/US Department of Health and Human Services.

Cover photographs reproduced with permission of Gareth Boden.

Every effort has been made to contact copyright holders of any material reproduced in this book. Any omissions will be rectified in subsequent printings if notice is given to the Publisher.

Some words in this book are in bold, **like this.** You can find out what they mean by looking in the glossary.

Contents

Key

* easy

** medium

*** difficult

Japanese Food

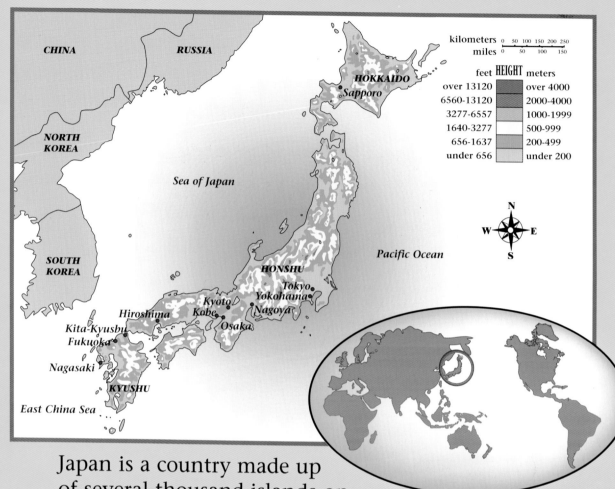

Japan is a country made up of several thousand islands on the western edge of the Pacific Ocean. Most people live on the largest island, called Honshu.

Japanese meals usually consist of rice, with a lot of small dishes to accompany it. Food is cooked very simply and lightly, so the taste of the natural ingredients comes through. Japanese people think that the way a dish looks is just as important as how it tastes.

In the past

Stone Age people settled in Japan more than 10,000 years ago. They lived by hunting, gathering, and fishing. From 660 B.C.E., Japan was ruled by emperors. In 1160 C.E., power passed to warriors called shoguns,

4

who banned most people from contact with the rest of the world. This **isolation** meant that no outside influences affected Japanese food.

By the end of the nineteenth century, Japan became more open and began to adopt some European and American ideas. After World War II ended in 1945, Western influences started to affect Japanese cooking.

▲ *Many Japanese people buy fresh food every day from stalls such as these.*

Around the country

The center of Japan is mountainous. Most people live in the flatter areas around the coast. Japan's climate varies widely from north to south. In the north, winters are cold and snowy, and summers are short. In the south, the climate is hot and **humid**.

Different crops are grown in different areas of Japan, but the main crop is rice. Other crops include barley, soybeans, sweet potatoes, tea, and citrus fruits. There are different food specialties around the country, too. Because most people in Japan live near the sea, fresh fish, seafood, and seaweed are popular ingredients.

Japanese meals

Traditionally, Japanese people don't have different foods for breakfast, lunch, and dinner. Nearly every meal includes soup and rice and perhaps three or four small vegetable, fish, or meat dishes. Desserts are rare.

Japanese food is usually eaten with chopsticks. Often, food is cut up into bite-sized pieces so that it can be easily picked up. See page 23 for how to use chopsticks.

Ingredients

Japanese cooking uses a lot of ingredients that may be unfamiliar outside Japan. You will find some in supermarkets and some in oriental or health food stores. This book suggests alternatives for ingredients that may be hard to find.

soy sauce

egg noodles

rice

tofu

sesame seeds

udon noodles

ginger

soba noodles

Dashi

Dashi is a liquid made from dried fish and seaweed. It is used in many dishes but is difficult to find outside Japan. If you can't find it, you can use vegetable **stock** instead.

Ginger

Peeled and **grated** fresh ginger is used in many Japanese dishes. It is readily available in supermarkets. It is better to use fresh rather than dried ginger, as it has more flavor.

Noodles

Noodles are very popular in Japan. There are many different types. Two of the most common types are *soba*—thin brown noodles and *udon*— thick white noodles. These noodles are sometimes sold in supermarkets, but if you cannot find them, use Chinese egg noodles, which are more widely available.

Rice

Rice is served at nearly every Japanese meal. Rice comes in three main types—short, medium, and long grain. Short grain rice is closer to the type of rice used in Japan.

Seaweed

Seaweed is used in many Japanese dishes. There are many different types. Three of the most common are *nori*—black seaweed—that is dried into sheets and used to wrap around rice, fish, and vegetables. *Kombu* is a dark-green seaweed, and *wakame* is a dark-green seaweed that is used in soups and salads. Seaweed is not an essential ingredient in this book.

nori seaweed

Sesame seeds

Sesame seeds are used to flavor many different Japanese dishes. **Toasting** them brings out their full flavor.

Soy sauce

Soy sauce is one of the most important ingredients in Japanese cooking and is used in nearly every dish. Soy sauce is called *shoyu* in Japanese and is made from soybeans, wheat, salt, and water.

Tofu

Tofu is made from **pulped** soybeans. It is also called bean curd. It can be found in most supermarkets.

Before You Begin

Kitchen rules

There are a few basic rules you should always follow when you cook:

- Ask an adult if you can use the kitchen.
- Some cooking processes, especially those involving hot water or oil, can be dangerous. When you see this sign, take extra care or ask an adult to help.
- Wash your hands before you begin.
- Wear an apron to protect your clothes. Tie back long hair.
- Be very careful when using sharp knives.
- Never leave pan handles sticking out—it could be dangerous if you bump into them.
- Always wear oven mitts when lifting things in and out of the oven.
- Wash fruits and vegetables before using them.

How long will it take?

Some of the recipes in this book are quick and easy, and some are more difficult and take longer. The strip across the top of the right-hand page of each recipe tells you how long it will take to cook the dish from start to finish. It also shows how difficult each dish is to make: * (easy), ** (medium), or *** (difficult).

Quantities and measurements

You can see how many people each recipe will serve at the top of the right-hand page, too. Most of the recipes in this book make enough to feed two people. A few of the recipes make enough for four. You can multiply or divide the quantities if you want to cook for more or fewer people.

Ingredients for recipes can be measured in two ways. Imperial measurements use cups, ounces, and fluid ounces. Metric measurements use grams and milliliters.

In the recipes you will see the following abbreviations:

tbsp = tablespoon   oz = ounce
tsp = teaspoon   lb = pound
ml = milliliters   cm = centimeters
g = gram

Utensils

To cook the recipes in this book, you will need these utensils, as well as kitchen essentials, such as a colander, spoons, plates, and bowls:

- cutting board
- chopsticks
- foil
- frying pan
- grater
- large, flat, ovenproof dish
- measuring cup
- metal or wooden skewers
- plastic lunch box
- roasting pan
- saucepan with lid
- set of measuring cups
- sharp knife
- colander
- small custard cups
- steamer (optional)
- baking sheet

! Whenever you use kitchen knives, be very careful.

9

Clear Soup

Many Japanese people eat soup for breakfast or before a formal meal. It is not eaten with a spoon—the idea is to pick out the solid ingredients with chopsticks, then pick up the bowl and drink the liquid.

What you need

1/2 carrot
1 green onion
1/4 lb (100 g) tofu
1/3 cup (50g) udon
   noodles (or Chinese
   egg noodles)
1 vegetable **bouillon
   cube**
2 tbsp soy sauce
1/3 tbsp granulated
   sugar

What you do

1 **Peel** the carrot and thinly **slice** it.

2 Cut the top and bottom off the green onion and finely **chop** the rest.

3 Cut the tofu into small pieces about 1/4 in. (1/2 cm) across.

4 Put 1 1/3 cups (270 ml) of water into a saucepan and bring it to a **boil**. Add the noodles, then turn the heat down and **simmer** for 4 minutes, until the noodles are soft.

(!) 5 **Drain** the water from the noodles using a colander. Put the noodles into two small bowls.

6 Pour 2 cups (500 ml) of water into a saucepan and bring it to a boil. Drop in the bouillon cube and stir until it **dissolves.** Turn the heat to simmer.

7 Add the sliced carrot, chopped green onion, tofu pieces, soy sauce, and sugar to the **stock.**

8 Simmer the stock for 5 minutes.

9 Carefully pour the stock over the noodles.

TRY THIS!

You can add many different ingredients to clear soup.
Try adding a small amount of the following:

- sliced mushrooms
- spinach
- sugar snap peas
- shrimp

You also could add wakame seaweed to clear soup. Soak the wakame in cold water for about 20 minutes, until it is soft. Then cut it into strips about 1/2 in (1 cm) wide and put it in the bowl with the noodles.

11

Custard

This **savory** custard is similar to a thick soup and is called *chawan mushi* in Japanese. It might be served at the end of a meal or as a snack. It is usually eaten hot but is sometimes served cold during the hot summer months.

What you need

1 vegetable **bouillon cube**
1/4 tbsp granulated sugar
1/2 tbsp soy sauce
2 eggs

What you do

1 Put 1 cup (200 ml) of water into a saucepan and bring it to a **boil.** Drop the bouillon cube into the water and stir until it **dissolves.** Turn the heat down to a **simmer.**

2 Add the sugar and soy sauce to the **stock.** Stir until the sugar dissolves.

3 Allow the stock to **cool** for about 15 minutes.

4 While the stock is cooling, crack the eggs into a bowl. **Beat** them with a fork or whisk until the yolk and white are mixed.

5 Pour the beaten eggs into the cooled stock, stirring gently as you pour.

6 Carefully pour the custard into two custard cups.

(!) 7 Put the custard cups in a steamer. Place the steamer over a pan of boiling water.

8 Turn the heat down to low. Put the lid on the steamer. **Steam** the custards for 30 minutes, until the mixture is **set**.

(!) 9 Wear an oven mitt to remove the hot custard cups from the steamer. Serve your custards in these dishes.

COOKING IN THE OVEN

If you don't have a steamer, you can cook the custards in the oven. **Preheat** the oven to 425°F (220°C). Fill a shallow roasting pan halfway with hot water and place the cups full of custard in the water. Make sure the cups are not floating. **Cover** the whole roasting pan with foil. Put the pan in the oven and cook the custards for 30 minutes.

TRY HUNTING!

Try adding other ingredients such as mushrooms or shrimp to the basic custard at step 6. You can hunt for the different ingredients when you eat the custard!

Grilled Tofu

The main religion in Japan is Buddhism. Buddhist temples often contain small restaurants that serve **vegetarian** food. Many of these dishes contain tofu. This grilled tofu dish is typical of the kind of food served in temples. You can serve it as an appetizer or snack.

What you need

1/3 lb (150 g) tofu
1 tbsp soy sauce
1 tbsp granulated
   sugar
1 tbsp lemon juice
1 tbsp sesame seeds

What you do

1 Cut the tofu into eight pieces about 1/2 in. (1.27 cm) thick.

2 Put the soy sauce, sugar, and lemon juice into a bowl. Add the tofu pieces and allow them to **marinate** for 1 hour.

(!) 3 While the tofu is marinating, put the sesame seeds into a frying pan without adding any oil. Heat the seeds over medium heat for about 5 minutes, keeping the pan moving, until the seeds are golden brown. Some may pop out, so use a splatter screen. Put the **toasted** sesame seeds aside.

4 When the tofu pieces are marinated, thread them onto skewers. If you use wooden skewers, soak them in water first.

5 Put the skewers on a baking sheet coated with cooking spray. **Broil** the tofu for 3 minutes on each side, until it is golden brown and cooked through.

6 Sprinkle the toasted sesame seeds onto the tofu.
Serve with a small dish of soy sauce for dunking.
Keep the tofu on the skewers and nibble it off!

WOODEN SKEWERS

If you don't have metal skewers, you can broil the tofu on
wooden skewers, which you can find at most supermarkets.
Soak the skewers in water for 10 minutes before using them
so they will not burn under the broiler.

Grilled Chicken

This grilled chicken dish is called *yakitori* in Japanese. Yakitori bars—small restaurants that serve only this dish—are found all over Japan.

What you need

2 boneless, skinless chicken breasts
2 tbsp soy sauce
1/2 tbsp granulated sugar

What you do

1 Cut the chicken breasts into cubes.

2 Mix the soy sauce and sugar in a large, flat dish. Put the chicken pieces into the sauce and turn to coat them. **Marinate** the chicken for 1 hour.

3 Thread the chicken pieces onto skewers. If you are using wooden skewers, soak them in water first.

(!) 4 Put the chicken skewers on a baking sheet coated with cooking spray. **Broil** the marinated chicken pieces for about 8 minutes on each side, until they are golden brown and cooked through.

VEGETARIAN SKEWERS

You can use vegetables instead of, or in addition to, chicken in this dish. Try pieces of zucchini, mushroom, or red pepper as shown below. You can even cook the skewers outside on a grill in the summer.

Chicken Soup

This soup is served as a main course in Japan. As with the clear soup on page 10, you eat the solid ingredients with chopsticks, then drink the liquid from the bowl.

What you need

2 tbsp soy sauce
2 tbsp granulated sugar
2 boneless, skinless chicken breasts
1 2/3 cups (250 g) udon noodles or Chinese egg noodles
1 vegetable **bouillon cube**
4 green onions

What you do

1 Mix the soy sauce and sugar in a large, flat dish.

2 Put the chicken breasts into the soy sauce and sugar mixture. Turn them over a couple of times until they are coated. Allow the chicken to **marinate** in the sauce for 1 hour.

3 When the chicken has marinated, place it on a baking sheet and **broil** for about 8 minutes on each side, until it is golden and cooked through.

(!) 4 Carefully take the chicken out of the broiler. Thinly **slice** it and put it aside.

5 Pour 2 1/2 cups (600 ml) of water into a saucepan and bring it to a **boil**. Drop the bouillon cube into the water and stir until it **dissolves.**

6 Add the noodles to the hot **stock.** Boil them for about 5 minutes, until they are soft.

7 Cut the tops and bottoms off the green onions and finely **chop** the rest.

(!) 8 Pour the noodles and stock into two bowls. Arrange the chicken slices and chopped green onions on top of the noodles.

Shrimp and Vegetable Stir-Fry

Food that is stirred while it is being fried over high heat makes a dish called a **stir-fry.** The ingredients in this traditional stir-fry are cooked very quickly, so the vegetables should still taste crunchy.

What you need

1/2 zucchini
3 large mushrooms
2 green onions
1/2 tbsp vegetable oil
1/3 lb (150 g) shrimp
1 1/3 cups (100 g)
   bean sprouts
1/2 tbsp lemon juice
1 tbsp soy sauce

What you do

1 **Slice** the zucchini and mushrooms.

2 Cut the tops and bottoms off the green onions and finely **chop** the rest.

(!) 3 Heat the oil in a frying pan over high heat.

4 Put the sliced zucchini and mushrooms, shrimp, and bean sprouts into the frying pan. **Fry** the ingredients on high heat, stirring all the time, for about 5 minutes.

5 Add the chopped green onion, lemon juice, and soy sauce to the frying pan and cook for another 2 minutes.

MORE STIR-FRY IDEAS

You can change this recipe to use all kinds of different ingredients. Try replacing the mushrooms and zucchini with other vegetables, such as:

- sliced carrots
- sugar snap peas
- pieces of broccoli

Chilled Noodles

In parts of Japan where summers are very hot, noodles are sometimes served cold. Dip each mouthful of noodles into the sauce before you eat it.

What you need

1 green onion
1 vegetable **bouillon cube**
1/4 cup (50 ml) soy sauce
1 tbsp granulated sugar
2/3 cup (100 g) soba noodles (or Chinese egg noodles)

What you do

1 Cut the top and bottom off the green onion and finely **chop** the rest.

2 Put 2/3 cup of water into a saucepan and bring it to a **boil**. Drop the bouillon cube into the water and stir until it **dissolves**.

3 Add the soy sauce, sugar, and chopped green onion to the **stock**. **Simmer** the sauce for 2 minutes, until the sugar has dissolved.

4 Carefully pour the sauce into two small dishes and allow to **cool**.

5 Pour 1 1/3 cups of water into a pan and bring it to a boil.

6 Add the noodles and cook them for about 5 minutes, until they are soft.

(!) 7 Pour the noodles into a colander. Rinse the noodles in cold water, then **drain** them and put them into two small dishes.

8 Give each person a dish of noodles and a dish of sauce.

HOW TO USE CHOPSTICKS

Pick up one chopstick and hold it between your thumb and first two fingers. This chopstick is the one that will move.

Put the second chopstick between your second and third fingers and behind your thumb. This chopstick stays still. Move the top chopstick up and down with your thumb and first finger so that the tips of the chopsticks meet.

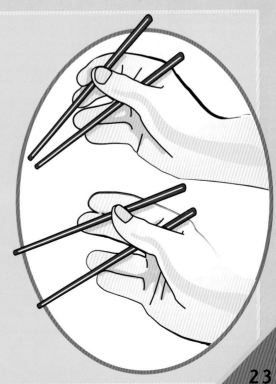

Salmon Teriyaki

Teriyaki is the Japanese name for a sauce made from soy sauce and sugar. Teriyaki sauce can be eaten with many different ingredients, such as fish, chicken, tofu, and vegetables.

What you need

4 large mushrooms
1/4 cup soy sauce
1 tbsp granulated
  sugar
1 tbsp vegetable oil
2/3 cup (50 g) bean
  sprouts
2 salmon steaks

What you do

1 **Slice** the mushrooms.

2 Put the soy sauce, sugar, and 2 tbsp water into a saucepan. Bring the mixture to a **boil**, then **simmer** for about 10 minutes, stirring all the time, until the sauce is thick and syrupy.

3 Remove the pan from the heat and put a lid on it to keep the sauce warm.

(!) 4 Heat the oil in a frying pan and add the sliced mushrooms and bean sprouts. **Fry** them for 5 minutes, then put them into an ovenproof dish.

5 Turn the oven on to its lowest setting and put the vegetables into the oven to keep them warm.

6 Put the salmon steaks into the frying pan. Cook them for about 5 minutes on each side, until they are slightly brown and cooked through.

7 Put one salmon steak and some of the cooked vegetables onto each plate. Carefully spoon the sauce over the salmon.

Beef Tataki

For this dish, the beef needs to **marinate** for at least 3 hours so that it can soak up all the flavors of the sauce. Start making it well before you want to eat it!

What you need

1/2 lb (225 g) steak
1 onion
1/2 tbsp lemon juice
1/4 cup (50 ml) white vinegar or malt vinegar
1/4 cup (50 ml) soy sauce
1 tbsp granulated sugar
lettuce leaves

What you do

1 **Broil** the steak for 15 minutes 6 in. (15 cm) from the heat, turning halfway through so that both sides are cooked.

2 While the steak is cooking, **peel** the onion and finely **chop** half of it.

3 Cut the steak in half to check that it is cooked all the way through. It should not be red.

4 Mix together the chopped onion, lemon juice, vinegar, soy sauce, and sugar in a bowl. Add the steak and coat it well with the **marinade.**

5 Leave the steak to marinate for at least 3 hours.

6 Remove the steak from the marinade and thinly **slice** it.

7 Arrange the lettuce leaves on two plates and place the beef slices on top.

EATING MEAT

Meat is thought of as quite a luxury in Japan, because it is very expensive. It is usually cut into thin slices and served with vegetables or salad, as in this dish.

Steamed Chicken with Broccoli

Most Japanese cooking is very healthy. This steamed chicken is particularly good for you because it is low in fat.

What you need

1/4 cup (50 ml) soy sauce
1/2 tbsp granulated sugar
2 boneless, skinless chicken breasts
6 broccoli flowerets

What you do

1 Mix the soy sauce and sugar in a bowl. Put the chicken into the bowl and allow to **marinate** in the refrigerator for 1 hour, turning once to coat the chicken with marinade.

(!) **2** Put the marinated chicken into a steamer over a saucepan of boiling water. Turn the heat down to low. **Steam** for 15 minutes, then turn the chicken over and steam for another 10 minutes.

3 Meanwhile, **chop** the broccoli flowerets into small pieces.

4 Bring a saucepan of water to a **boil.** Add the broccoli and cook for 5 minutes.

(!) **5** Carefully take the chicken breasts out of the steamer with a fork. Put them onto a cutting board. **Slice** them about 1/4 in. (1/2 cm) thick.

6 Arrange the chicken slices and broccoli on two plates.

COOKING IN THE OVEN

If you don't have a steamer, you can cook the chicken in the oven. **Preheat** the oven to 400°F (200°C). Put the chicken into an ovenproof dish. Fill a roasting pan halfway with hot water, then carefully place the dish with the chicken in it into the water. **Cover** the roasting pan with foil. Put the pan in the oven and cook the chicken for 30 minutes.

Tuna and Egg Rice Bowl

Japanese cooking uses a lot of fish and seafood. This tuna dish makes an ideal lunch or snack.

What you need

1 1/4 cup (200 g)
   short-grain rice
1 6-oz (150-g) can tuna
1 **bouillon cube**
1 onion
1/2 tbsp soy sauce
1/2 tbsp granulated sugar
1 egg

What you do

1 Put the rice into a colander. Hold the colander under cold running water and rinse the rice until the water runs clear.

2 Put the rinsed rice into a saucepan and add 1 2/3 (325 ml) cups of water. Put a lid on the pan. Bring the water to a **boil**, then lower the heat and **simmer** the rice for about 20 minutes, or until it has soaked up all the water.

3 Put the cooked rice into two small bowls.

4 **Drain** the tuna by emptying it into a colander and letting the liquid drain away.

5 Put the drained tuna into a bowl. Use a fork to break it up into small pieces.

6 Put 1/2 cup (100 ml) of water into a saucepan and bring it to a boil. Drop the bouillon cube into the water and stir until it **dissolves**.

7 **Peel** and **chop** half the onion. Carefully add the chopped onion to the **stock** and simmer for 5 minutes, until the onion is soft.

8 Add the tuna, soy sauce, and sugar to the stock. Simmer for 2 minutes.

(!) 9 Spoon the stock from the pan over the bowls of rice, leaving the tuna and onions in the pan.

10 Crack the egg into a small bowl. **Beat** the egg with a fork or whisk until the yolk and white are mixed.

11 Pour the beaten egg over the tuna and onions. Put a lid on the pan and cook for 3 minutes.

12 Spoon the tuna and egg mixture onto the rice.

Rice Balls

Rice balls are the Japanese version of sandwiches. They often are put into packed lunches or taken on picnics. In this recipe, the rice balls are made in small bowls.

What you need

1 1/4 cup (200 g) short-grain rice

1/4 cup (50 g) canned tuna

1 onion

1/2 tbsp granulated sugar

1 tbsp soy sauce

What you do

1 Pour the rice into a colander. Pu the colander under cold running water and rinse the rice until the water runs clear.

2 Put the rinsed rice into a saucepa and add 1 2/3 (325 ml) cups of water. Put a lid on the pan. Bring the water to a **boil**, then lower the heat and **simmer** the rice for about 20 minutes, or until the rice has soaked up all the water.

3 **Drain** the tuna by emptying it into a colander and letting the liquid drain away.

4 Put the drained tuna into a bowl. Use a fork to break it up into small pieces

5 **Peel** the onion and finely **chop** half of it.

6 Put the sugar, soy sauce, and choppe onion into a saucepan over medium heat.

7 Cook the mixture, stirring all the tim until the sugar has **dissolved** and the onion is soft.

8 Add the tuna to the saucepan and cook for another 5 minutes.

9 Put 2 tbsp of the rice into a small bowl. Make a well in the middle of the rice and spoon 1 tsp of the tuna mixture into the well. Then put 1 tsp of rice on top and shape the rice into a ball with the spoon.

10 Repeat this process until you have used all the rice and tuna mixture. You should have enough to fill four to six small bowls.

11 Allow the rice balls to **cool**. Serve them in the bowls or lift them all out onto a large plate.

NORIMAKI

In Japan, rice often is wrapped in seaweed and rolled up. These rolls are called *norimaki*. To make them, seaweed is cooked, the filling spooned onto it, and the nori rolled up into a tube. The tube is then sliced to make norimaki.

Grilled Zucchini with Ginger

This vegetable dish is simple to make. You can either serve it as a main course or as a side dish.

What you need

2 zucchini
1/2 vegetable **bouillon cube**
1 tbsp soy sauce
1/2 tbsp granulated sugar
1 small piece fresh ginger, 1 in. (2.5 cm) long

What you do

1 With a sharp knife, cut the ends off the zucchini, then cut the rest in half lengthwise.

2 **Peel** the ginger and either **grate** or finely **chop** it.

3 Arrange the zucchini halves, skin side down, on a baking sheet. **Broil** them for 5 minutes, until they begin to brown.

4 Turn the zucchini halves over, so the skin faces up. Broil for another 5 minutes.

5 Put 1/4 cup of water into a saucepan and bring it to a **boil**. Drop the 1/2 bouillon cube into the water and stir until it **dissolves**.

6 Add the soy sauce and sugar to the **stock** and **simmer** for 5 minutes.

7 Arrange the zucchini halves onto plates, then pour the sauce over them.

8 Sprinkle the grated or chopped ginger over the zucchini.

EGGPLANT ALTERNATIVE

You can try making this dish with eggplants instead of zucchinis. Cut the eggplants into slices, then broil them for 10 minutes on each side.

Sweet Potatoes with Soy Sauce

This side dish goes well with most of the main courses in this book, especially steamed chicken with broccoli, beef tataki, and salmon teriyaki.

What you need

2 sweet potatoes
1/3 cup (75 g) granulated sugar
2 tbsp soy sauce

What you do

1 **Peel** the sweet potatoes, then slice them about 3/4 in. (2 cm) thick.

2 Put the slices of sweet potato into a saucepan. Add enough water to nearly cover them.

3 Add the sugar and **cover** the pan.

4 Bring the water to a **boil**, then **simmer** for about 15 minutes, until the potatoes are soft.

(!) 5 Pour the potatoes into a colander and **drain** the water from them. Put the potatoes in a bowl, then sprinkle them with the soy sauce.

YAKI-IMO!

In Japan, baked sweet potatoes, or *yaki-imo*, are often sold on the street. They are baked over fires or on hot stones and are particularly popular during the cold Japanese winters. The yaki-imo seller pushes a cart through the streets calling out, "Yaki-imo!" to attract customers.

Green Beans with Sesame Seeds

Sesame seeds often are used as part of a dressing or sauce in Japanese cooking. They go very well with the beans in this recipe.

What you need

1/4 lb (100 g) green beans
1 tbsp sesame seeds
1/2 tbsp granulated sugar
1/2 tbsp soy sauce

What you do

1 Cut the stalk ends off the green beans, then cut them into 2 in.(5 cm) long pieces.

(!) 2 Fill a saucepan with water and bring it to a **boil**. Add the beans and cook for 2 minutes. **Drain** the beans into a colander, then put them into a large bowl.

(!) 3 Put the sesame seeds into a frying pan without adding any oil. **Toast** them over medium heat for about 5 minutes, tossing them from time to time, until they are golden brown. Use a splatter screen to keep seeds from popping out!

4 Mix the toasted sesame seeds, sugar, soy sauce, and 1/2 tbsp water in a small bowl.

5 Pour the dressing over the beans.

CABBAGE LEAVES

This sesame seed dressing can be used with
other vegetables. Try cooking some Chinese cabbage leaves
by carefully lowering them into boiling water for about
1 minute, draining them, then pouring the sesame seed
dressing over them.

Toffee Sweet Potatoes

What you need

1/2 lb (225 g) sweet
   potatoes
1/3 cup (75 g)
   granulated sugar
1 tbsp sesame seeds

Traditional Japanese food does not include many desserts. However, Japanese people sometimes eat cakes and other sweet dishes as a snack with a cup of tea.

What you do

1 **Peel** the sweet potatoes and **slice** them about 3/4 in. (2 cm) thick.

2 Put the sesame seeds into a frying pan without adding any oil. **Toast** them over medium heat for about 5 minutes, tossing them from time to time, until they are golden brown. Watch out for hot seeds popping out! Put the toasted sesame seeds aside.

3 Put the slices of sweet potato into a saucepan and cover them with water.

4 Bring the water to a **boil**, then **simmer** the potatoes for 10 minutes, until they are just beginning to go soft.

5 **Drain** the potatoes into a colander and put them aside.

6 Put the sugar into a pan with 1/4 cup (25 ml) of water and bring the mixture to a boil. Boil it for about 7 minutes, without stirring, until the mixture turns into a light-brown syrup.

⊘ 7 Add the cooked sweet potato slices to the warm syrup, turning them so that they are well coated. Sprinkle them with the toasted sesame seeds.

8 Put a sheet of wax paper onto a plate. Take the potatoes out of the pan, one by one, and lay them on the paper.

9 Allow the toffee syrup to harden.

GREEN TEA

Green tea is very popular in Japan. Green tea is enjoyed plain, without milk or sugar. Green tea has become much more common in the West in the last few years and can be found in most supermarkets.

Japanese Lunch Box

Lunch boxes, known as *bento,* are very common in Japan. People take lunch boxes to work or school, but they also are sold at railroad stations, theaters, and restaurants.

You can put many of the foods in this book into your lunch box. Lunch boxes are a good way of using up any leftovers from your Japanese cooking. You can use the following recipes from this book:

- grilled tofu (page 14)
- grilled chicken (page 16)
- salmon teriyaki (page 24)
- beef tataki (page 26)
- steamed chicken with broccoli (page 28)
- rice balls (page 32)
- sweet potatoes with soy sauce (page 36)
- green beans with sesame seeds (page 38)
- toffee sweet potatoes (page 40)

Some Japanese lunch boxes also include fresh fruit.

ROLLED OMELETTE

Here is a quick and easy recipe that's ideal to go in a lunch box. Make one omelette for each person.

What you need

2 eggs
1 tbsp soy sauce
1/2 tsp granulated
   sugar
1/2 tbsp vegetable oil

What you do

1 Crack the eggs into a small bowl. **Beat** them with a fork or whisk until the yolk and white are mixed. Add the soy sauce and sugar and mix well.

(!) **2** Heat the oil in a frying pan over medium heat. Pour in the egg and tilt the pan so that the mixture spreads evenly over the bottom of the pan.

3 Cook the omelette for about 5 minutes, until it is set.

4 Tip the omelette onto a cutting board. Wait for it to cool for a minute or two. Roll the omelette up into a tube shape and allow it to cool for at least 5 more minutes.

5 When it is cool, **slice** the omelette into 3/4-in. (2-cm) pieces.

More Books

Cookbooks

Ridgewell, Jenny. *A Taste of Japan.* Austin, Tex.: Raintree Steck Vaughn, 1993.

Takeshita, Jiro. *Food in Japan.* Vero Beach, Fla.: The Rourke Book Co., 1989.

Weston, Reiko. *Cooking the Japanese Way.* Minneapolis, Minn.: Lerner Publications, 1989.

Books About Japan

Martin, Fred. *Next Stop Japan.* Chicago, Ill.: Heinemann Library, 1998.

Witherick, Michael. *Japan.* Chicago, Ill.: Heinemann Library, 2000.

Comparing Weights and Measures

3 teaspoons = 1 tablespoon	1 tablespoon = 1/2 fluid ounce	1 teaspoon = 5 milliliters
4 tablespoons = 1/4 cup	1 cup = 8 fluid ounces	1 tablespoon = 15 milliliters
5 1/3 tablespoons = 1/3 cup	1 cup = 1/2 pint	1 cup = 240 milliliters
8 tablespoons = 1/2 cup	2 cups = 1 pint	1 quart = 1 liter
10 2/3 tablespoons = 2/3 cup	4 cups = 1 quart	1 ounce = 28 grams
12 tablespoons = 3/4 cup	2 pints = 1 quart	1 pound = 454 grams
16 tablespoons = 1 cup	4 quarts = 1 gallon	

Healthy Eating

This diagram shows which foods you should eat to stay healthy. You should eat 6–11 servings a day of foods from the bottom of the pyramid. Eat 2–4 servings of fruits and 3–5 servings of vegetables a day. You should also eat 2–3 servings from the milk group and 2–3 servings from the meat group. Eat only a few of the foods from the top of the pyramid.

Noodles, rice, fish, tofu, and vegetables are main ingredients, so Japanese cooking is very healthy. Fats, oils, and sweets are a very small part of a normal Japanese diet.

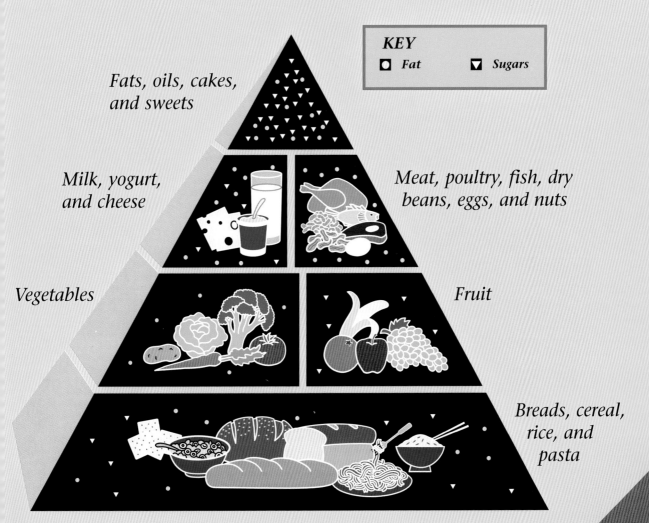

Fats, oils, cakes, and sweets

KEY
◻ *Fat*   ▽ *Sugars*

Milk, yogurt, and cheese

Meat, poultry, fish, dry beans, eggs, and nuts

Vegetables

Fruit

Breads, cereal, rice, and pasta

Glossary

beat to mix something together strongly, for example egg yolks and whites

boil to cook a liquid on the stovetop until it bubbles and steams strongly

bouillon cube small cube of powdered vegetable or meat flavoring used to make a base for soups or sauces

broil to cook something over or under an open flame

chop to cut something into pieces with a knife

cool to allow hot food to become cold, especially before putting it in the refrigerator.

cover to put a lid on a pan or foil over a dish

dissolve to stir something, such as sugar, until it disappears into a liquid

drain to remove liquid from a pan or can of food

fry to cook something by placing it in hot oil or fat

grate to shred something by rubbing it back and forth over a utensil that has a rough surface

humid climate that is hot and wet

isolated cut off from other people or the rest of the world

marinate to soak something, such as meat or fish, in a mixture before cooking so that it absorbs the taste of the mixture

peel to remove the skin of a fruit or vegetable

preheat to turn on the oven in advance, so that it is hot when you are ready to use it

pulp mixture that has been mashed until smooth

savory dish that is not sweet

set to become firm after chilling or baking

simmer to cook a liquid gently on the stovetop just under a boil

slice to cut something into thin, flat pieces

steam to cook a food by letting it sit in the steam coming from boiling water

stir-fry to quickly cook foods over high heat, stirring all the time

stock broth made by slowly cooking meat or vegetables in water or by dissolving a cube of powdered meat flavoring in water

toasted heated in a pan without any oil

vegetarian diet that usually does not include meat, poultry, or fish and that sometimes does not include eggs or dairy products; person who follows such a diet

Index